T0123215

THE
ARTIST'S
DATE BOOK

Also by Julia Cameron

ILLUSTRATED BY ELIZABETH CAMERON EVANS

THE
ARTIST'S
DATE BOOK

A COMPANION VOLUME TO
THE ARTIST'S WAY
by
JULIA CAMERON

JEREMY P. TARCHER/PUTNAM
A MEMBER OF PENGUIN PUTNAM INC.
NEW YORK

Jeremy P. Tarcher/Putnam
a member of
Penguin Putnam Inc.
375 Hudson Street
New York, NY 10014
www.penguinputnam.com

Library of Congress Cataloging-in-Publication Data

Cameron, Julia.
The artist's date book : a companion volume to The artist's way /
Julia Cameron ; illustrated by Elizabeth Cameron Evans.
p.   cm.
ISBN 978-0-87477-653-9
ISBN 0-87477-653-8
1. Creative ability—Problems, exercises, etc.   2. Self-actualization (Psychology)—
Problems, exercises, etc.   3. Creation (Literary, artistic, etc.).
I. Evans, Elizabeth Cameron.   II. Cameron, Julia. Artist's way.   III. Title.
BF408.C174   1999   99-29066 CIP
153.3′5—dc21

Book design by Claire Naylon Vaccaro
and Deborah Kerner

Acknowledgments

I wish to thank my sister Libby, whose art has been a lifelong source of enjoyment for me and my family. I also wish to thank my parents, James and Dorothy, whose love of *New Yorker* cartoons and James Thurber made wit a part of the way I witnessed life.

JULIA CAMERON

I dedicate these drawings to my wonderful husband, Gary, with whose love, encouragement, and humor my art and life have been immeasurably enriched. Also with gratitude and love to our dear family and friends, and with love forever to my animal teachers: Peri, Wolf, Alice, Angel, Chico, Sweetie, Saudi, Baron, Domino, Kingy, Woody, Skippy, Karma the 14th, and Roy-El's Faeritale. And finally, to magical, kind, and lovely Julie, who is like having Pegasus for a sister.

ELIZABETH "Libby" CAMERON EVANS

We dedicate this book
to our family.

INTRODUCTION

Eighteen years ago, I encountered a cartoon character named Theo. Drawn by my sister Libby, a portrait artist, Theo engaged in all sorts of adventures that bore little resemblance to "fine art." Theo watched snowflakes, dazzled. Theo went sledding in the middle of his work day. Theo wore Hawaiian shirts at Christmas. Theo had a good time.

"Where did Theo come from?" I asked Libby.

"Oh, Theo is what happens when you try to shoehorn someone creative into corporate life."

In teaching creative recovery, I have often heard the sentence "Julia, I know I need to work on my creativity." It's that word "work" that sends my alarm bells ringing. I want to say, "Work is the problem. Play is the solution." As blocked creatives, most of us have learned very well how to keep our nose to the grindstone, how to make our days gray, drab, and colorless. What we need, I have often thought, is a little dose of Theo.

There are two bedrock tools essential to any creative recovery. The first of these tools involves work. This tool is the Morning Pages—three pages of private, daily, longhand writing, shown to no one but our own creative selves. In order to do Morning Pages, people must get up even earlier, restructure their day, marshal their energies, and march to the page. In my experience, people do Morning Pages easily, even eagerly. We do, as I have said, understand work.

Now to the second tool, the sticky one. The second primary tool of a creative recovery involves play. Oh, this tool is hard to master. Dubbed an "Artist Date," this second, essential tool involves a once-weekly, solitary, festive expedition targeted at enticing our inner artist into exploring new realms. Students who willingly rise at five-thirty to take to the page balk, cavil, whine, and rebel at the prospect of taking in, say, a solo movie, a visit to an art supply shop, a trip to the park, a jaunt to Chinatown.

"You are building a radio kit," I explain patiently. "With Morning Pages you are sending. Telling the Universe what you would like more of, what you would like less of, what would move you closer to your dreams. When you take an Artist Date, you are setting the dial to receive. Now you hear hunches, inspiration, guidance. As your inner listening improves, you experience increased synchronicity. More and more often, you are in the right place at the right time."

Say what I will, Artist Dates remain difficult. So I try again.

"Art is an image-using system," I tell my students. "Think of yourself as having an inner trout pond, filled with images.

When you use your creativity, you are drawing on this inner well. When you draw on it heavily, you will overfish your pond unless you learn to consciously replenish your store of images. Taking your Artist Date restocks the pond."

Students will say, "Julia, I was writing like a bat out of hell and suddenly it dried up. Why?"

I will answer, "It dried up because you were writing well, because you were writing like a bat out of hell. Anytime you are working intensely, you should double your Artist Dates."

"But, Julia! When I'm working well, all I want to do is work."

I understand. It is because I understand the difficulty of taking Artist Dates that I have enlisted the help of Theo and Libby in making this book. For two decades, Libby has endured being a creative guinea pig for my practices. As one of my earliest *Artist's Way* "victims," she has had years to think up Artist Dates and face down her own inner resistance. An internationally noted portrait artist, with a specialty in canine and equine art, she has maintained the guilty pleasure of her secret life as a cartoonist. Throughout the years, Theo has insisted on having his say.

The book you hold in your hands functions on several levels. In Theo's cartoon life, the key principles of *The Artist's Way* and creative recovery are cartooned and clarified. Each page contains a few lines for your responses to the cartoon, or for your personal use, in listing the day's creative priorities. You will find a small check-in box to monitor your progress with both your Morning Pages and your Artist Dates. At page bottom, you will find a festive suggestion for an Artist Date. There are three hundred and sixty-five pages in this book. Start your year where you are, and allow Theo to wag his tail.

It is my hope you will find this book an enjoyable companion and a practical guide to the practice of creative self-nurturing.

— JULIA CAMERON

DAY 1

NO MATTER WHAT LIFE PATH YOU ARE ON, IT IS NEVER TOO LATE TO WORK ON YOUR CREATIVITY

GO TO A PARK.

DAY 2

EACH OF US IS COMPLEX AND
HIGHLY INDIVIDUAL—

YET THERE ARE COMMON RECOG-
NIZABLE DENOMINATORS TO THE
CREATIVE RECOVERY PROCESS.

_____

_____

_____

_____

_____

_____

AKE A PORTRAIT GALLERY OF YOUR FRIENDS.

DAY 3

WE ARE
OURSELVES
CREATIONS
AND WE
IN TURN
ARE MEANT
TO
CONTINUE
CREATIVITY
BY
BEING
CREATIVE
OURSELVES.

_____

_____

_____

_____

_____

_____

_____

_____

_____

DRAW ON WHISKERS.

DAY 4

UNFORTUNATELY, MANY
ARTISTS NEVER RECEIVE
CRITICAL EARLY
ENCOURAGEMENT.

_____
_____
_____
_____
_____
_____
_____
_____
_____

WRITE A LULLABY.

DAY 5

FOR MOST OF US THE IDEA THAT THE CREATOR ENCOURAGES CREATIVITY IS A RADICAL THOUGHT.

LISTEN TO MOZART.

DAY 6

Recovery is the process of finding the river and saying yes to its flow, rapids and all.

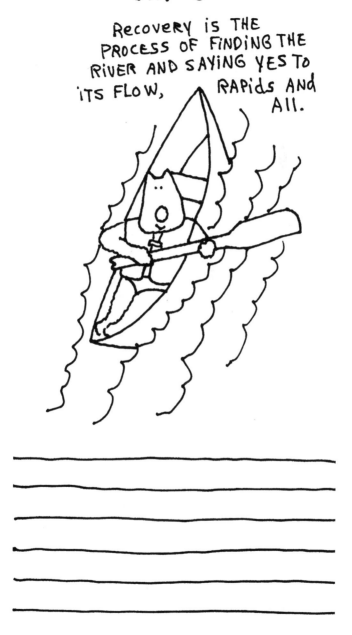

_____
_____
_____
_____
_____
_____

GET A NEW TOOTHBRUSH.

DAY 7

IT IS SAFE TO OPEN OUR-SELVES UP TO GREATER AND GREATER CREATIVITY.

BUY A SKETCHBOOK.

DAY 8

CREATIVITY IS GOD ENERGY FLOWING THROUGH US, SHAPED BY US, LIKE LIGHT FLOWING THROUGH A CRYSTAL PRISM.

MAKE AN ARTIST'S ALTAR.

DAY 9

AS WE OPEN OUR CREATIVE CHANNEL TO THE CREATOR, MANY GENTLE BUT POWERFUL CHANGES ARE TO BE EXPECTED.

LISTEN TO FLUTE MUSIC.

DAY 10

WHEN WE OPEN OUR-SELVES TO OUR CREATIV-ITY, WE OPEN OUR-SELVES TO THE CREATOR'S CREATIVITY WITHIN US AND OUR LIVES.

WRITE YOUR IDEAL DAY.

DAY 11

THE "STILL, SMALL VOICE"
IS AMPLIFIED WHEN WE
GO INSIDE TO HEAR IT.

_____

_____

_____

_____

_____

_____

_____

SPEND A DAY IN SILENCE.

DAY 12

MORNING PAGES ARE THREE
PAGES OF DAILY MORNING WRITING
ABOUT ABSOLUTELY ANYTHING.

_____

_____

_____

_____

_____

_____

BUY A GLITTER PEN.

DAY 13

TAKE A NAP.

DAY 14

THERE IS
NO WRONG
WAY TO DO
MORNING
PAGES.

DO A HEAD STAND.

DAY 15

MORNING PAGES MAP
OUR OWN INTERIOR.

BUY A GLOBE.

DAY 16

DO NOT JUDGE YOURSELF OR YOUR MORNING PAGES.

WRITE A TABLOID STORY.

DAY 17

MORNING PAGES
MAKE A WORD
TRAIL INWARD
TO THE SELF.

BUY WALKING SHOES.

DAY 18

DANG[ER]
SHORTCUT
CLARITY
SWITCHBACK

THROUGH
MORNING
PAGES
WE SEE WHAT
OBSTACLES IMPEDE
US, WHAT ROADS
ARE OPEN TO US.

TAKE A TRAIN RIDE.

DAY 19

BY
SPilliNG
OUT OF
BED AND
STRAIGHT ONTO
THE PAGE EVERY
MORNING, YOU
LEARN TO EVADE
THE CENSOR.

BUY NEW SHEETS.

DAY 20

THE MORNING PAGES MINIATURIZE OUR CENSOR.

WEAR A COLOR THAT IS NEW TO YOU.

DAY 21

MORNING PAGES WILL WORK FOR ANYONE WHO WANTS TO TRY ANY-THING CREATIVE.

DRESS UP YOUR PET.

DAY 22

THROUGH THE MORNING PAGES
YOU WILL ENCOUNTER THE
PROPULSION OF CREATIVE
FLOW UNDERLYING AND
INFORMING ALL OF LIFE.

TAKE A CANDLELIGHT BATH.

DAY 23

MORNING PAGES ARE LIKE GETTING UP IN THE MORNING AND TELEPHONING YOURSELF.

_____

_____

_____

_____

_____

_____

_____

_____

SING SCALES.

DAY 24

WITH MORNING PAGES
WE BECOME EXPLORERS
RATHER THAN MERE TOURISTS.

GO TO THE BEACH.

DAY 25

GET THAT PILE OF
RANDOM THOUGHTS OUT
OF YOUR HEAD AND ONTO
THOSE 3 MORNING PAGES!

MAKE A SAND CASTLE.

DAY 26

NO WONDER MY HEAD FELT SO CROWDED.
All THE CIRCUITS WERE FUll.

_____
_____
_____
_____
_____
_____
_____
_____

GO BIKE RIDING.

DAY 27

WITH MORNING PAGES IT IS
AS THOUGH YOU HAVE BUILT
A RADIO KIT AND ARE SENDING.

_____

_____

_____

_____

_____

_____

SEND POSTCARDS TO FIVE FRIENDS.

DAY 28

COLLAGE YOUR CREATIVE DREAM.

DAY 29

_____

_____

_____

_____

_____

_____

_____

_____

_____

"I FEEL O.K." IS A
BLANKET STATEMENT.
WE NEED TO GET SPECIFIC
IN OUR MORNING PAGES.

_____

_____

_____

_____

_____

_____

_____

_____

_____

LIST 50 THINGS YOU LOVE.

DAY 30

GLITTER A PLASTIC TOY.

DAY 31

YES SHE DID SAY MORNING
PAGES MUST BE DONE IN
LOOOOONG HAND.

_____

_____

_____

_____

_____

_____

_____

_____

CHANGE YOUR MAKEUP.

DAY 32

THE CHANNEL CHALLENGE!

AS WE BEGIN TO PRY OURSELVES LOOSE FROM OUR OLD SELF-CONCEPTS, WE FIND THAT OUR NEW, EMERGING SELF MAY ENJOY All SORTS OF BIZARRE ADVENTURES.

PET A LIZARD.

DAY 33

AN ARTIST DATE IS A ONCE-
WEEKLY FESTIVE, SOLITARY,
EXPLORATORY OUTING.

_____

_____

_____

_____

_____

_____

BUY BALLOONS.

DAY 34

COME PLAY.

WRITE A STORY ABOUT YOUR DOG.

DAY 35

FlAMENCO lessons
MiGHT BE FUN.

_____
_____
_____
_____
_____
_____
_____
_____

GO SEE LiVE MUSiC.

DAY 36

FIRST YOU SEE A FRENCH
FILM ON AN ARTIST DATE...

COMPLIMENT 5 STRANGERS.

DAY 37

THEN YOU TAKE A CLASS
ON THE FRENCH
IMPRESSIONISTS...

LEARN TO MAKE PAPIER-MÂCHÉ.

DAY 38

THEN YOU GO TO FRANCE.

_____

_____

_____

_____

_____

_____

_____

_____

EXPERIMENT WITH A NEW FOOD.

DAY 39

BY DOING YOUR ARTIST DATE,
YOU ARE RECEIVING—
OPENING YOURSELF TO
INSIGHT, INSPIRATION,
GUIDANCE.

WRITE A PRAYER.

DAY 40

TAKE
YOUR
ARTIST
ON A
SKATE
DATE.

GO ICE-SKATING.

DAY 41

BUY NEW LINGERIE.

DAY 42

STARGAZING IS
GOOD FOR YOU.

DESIGN YOUR OWN DECK OF CARDS.

DAY 43

ART GIVES US TIME TO LOOK AT THE WORLD CLOSE UP.

_____

_____

_____

_____

_____

_____

_____

_____

_____

_____

_____

PHOTOGRAPH YOUR PET.

DAY 44

HEY THEO, I GUESS THOSE ARTIST DATES ARE GOING REALLY WELL!?

MAKE A VALENTINE ANY TIME OF YEAR

DAY 45

———————————
———————————
———————————
———————————
———————————
———————————
———————————
———————————
———————————

Theo PoTTer

————————————————————
————————————————————
————————————————————
————————————————————
————————————————————
————————————————————
————————————————————
————————————————————

TAKE A POTTERY CLASS.

DAY 46

AN ARTIST REQUIRES THE UPKEEP OF CREATIVE SOLITUDE, THE HEALING OF TIME ALONE. WITHOUT THIS PERIOD OF RECHARGING, WE BECOME DEPLETED.

PLAY SOLITAIRE.

DAY 47

WE NEED TO REPLENISH OUR INNER
POND. AS ARTISTS, WE MUST LEARN
TO BE SELF-NOURISHING.

_____

_____

_____

_____

_____

_____

_____

BURN A SCENTED CANDLE.

DAY 48

Do what you love.

GO PET A HORSE.

DAY 49

BEING AN ARTIST REQUIRES
ENTHUSIASM MORE THAN
Discipline.

_____

_____

_____

_____

_____

_____

SING IN THE SHOWER.

DAY 50

SHAKE...!

TAKE A DANCE CLASS.

DAY 51

RATTLE...!

DANCE TO THE BEATLES SOLO.

DAY 52

Roll...!

CHA CHA.

DAY 53

Theo enters the sea of creativity with some trepidation....

USS CREATIVE

BUY LUCKY SOCKS.

DAY 54

the mythology is :

artists are drunks

DRINK A CHOCOLATE MALTED.

DAY 55

NoveL Beaujolais

MAKE CIDER.

DAY 56

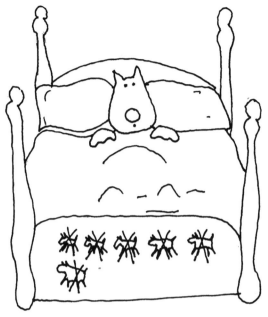

ARTISTS ARE PROMISCUOUS?

_____
_____
_____
_____
_____
_____
_____

GET A MASSAGE.

DAY 57

NEGATIVE BELIEF:
ARTISTS CAN'T AFFORD
FAMILIES.

_____

_____

_____

_____

_____

_____

_____

_____

_____

_____

WRITE A CHILDREN'S STORY.

DAY 58

artist=con man

WEAR A FAKE TATTOO.

DAY 59

WE TEND TO THINK, OR AT LEAST FEAR, THAT CREATIVE DREAMS ARE EGOTISTICAL, SOMETHING GOD WOULDN'T APPROVE OF FOR US.

THROW AWAY YOUR LOW-SELF-WORTH CLOTHING.

DAY 60

FEAR: I will ABANDON
FRIENDS AND FAMILY.

_____
_____
_____
_____
_____
_____
_____
_____

HAVE SOMEONE TO TEA.

DAY 61

MAKE JELL-O.

DAY 62

FEAR: FRIENDS & FAMILY WILL HATE
ME & PUSH ME AWAY.

_____

_____

_____

_____

_____

_____

_____

_____

_____

_____

MAKE A PHOTO ALBUM.

DAY 63

FEAR: IS A "CRAZY" ARTIST INSIDE ME?

DRESS UP FOR NO REASON.

DAY 64

FEAR: I'll NEVER HAVE ANY REAL $.

LIST 100 PEOPLE YOU LOVE.

DAY 65

FEAR:
I CAN'T BE
AN ARTIST,
I WILL FEEL
TOO ANGRY.

_____
_____
_____
_____
_____
_____
_____
_____
_____

READ A JOKE BOOK.

DAY 66

FEAR: THE INTELLECTUALS
will **LAUGH** AT MY WORK.
I will MELT.

_____

_____

_____

_____

_____

_____

_____

_____

PUT STICK-ON STARS ON YOUR CEILING.

DAY 67

FEAR OF SPELLING IS NOT TOO DUMB TO MENTION...
INTERNALIZED NEGATIVITY IS VERY EFFECTIVE WEAPONRY...

WRITE A COUNTRY-WESTERN SONG.

DAY 68

IT IS <u>ALWAYS</u> FEAR, OFTEN DISGUISED BUT ALWAYS THERE, THAT LEADS US INTO GRABBING FOR A BLOCK.

_____

_____

_____

_____

_____

_____

SELECT A GOD JAR

DAY 69

THE REFUSAL TO BE
CREATIVE IS COUNTER
TO OUR TRUE NATURE.

GLITTER YOUR SNEAKERS.

DAY 70

EACH OF US IS A UNIQUE
CREATIVE INDIVIDUAL.

_____
_____
_____
_____
_____
_____
_____

MAKE YOUR OWN PUZZLE.

DAY 71

IT IS AS THOUGH ALL THE STORIES, PAINTINGS, MUSIC, PERFORMANCES IN THE WORLD LIVE JUST UNDER THE SURFACE OF OUR NORMAL CONSCIOUSNESS.

LIST 5 MOVIES YOU'D LIKE TO MAKE.

DAY 72

AS I
CREATE
AND
LISTEN
I will
Be Led.

MAKE A DRUM.

DAY 73

THERE IS
A DIVINE
PLAN OF
GOODNESS
FOR MY WORK.

_____
_____
_____
_____
_____
_____
_____
_____

TAKE A LONG WALK.

DAY 74

I AM WILLING TO
EXPERIENCE MY
CREATIVE ENERGY.

DRESS LIKE A ROCK STAR.

DAY 75

A STRONGER AND CLEARER ME IS EMERGING.

WRITE A LOVE LETTER TO YOURSELF.

DAY 76

IT IS POSSIBLE, QUITE
POSSIBLE, TO BE BOTH
AN ARTIST AND
ROMANTICALLY
FULFILLED.

_____
_____
_____
_____
_____
_____
_____

GO TO A CHOCOLATE SHOP.

DAY 77

WHEN WE OPEN OURSELVES
TO EXPLORING OUR
CREATIVITY, WE OPEN
OURSELVES TO God:
good orderly direction.

_____

_____

_____

_____

_____

_____

VISIT A SACRED SPACE.

DAY 78

I AM A CHANNEL FOR
God's CREATIVITY AND
MY WORK COMES TO GOOD.

_____

_____

_____

_____

_____

_____

_____

DESIGN A GREETING CARD.

DAY 79

USING OUR CREATIVITY
IS OUR GIFT BACK
TO GOd.

WRITE A THANK-YOU NOTE.

DAY 80

I AM WILLING TO LET
GOD CREATE THROUGH ME.

SPEAK IN RHYME.

DAY 81

MY DREAMS
COME FROM
God.

_____

_____

_____

_____

_____

_____

_____

_____

_____

SEW BELLS ON THE TOES
OF YOUR SLEEP SOCKS.

DAY 82

I NEED TO CREATE
WHAT WANTS TO BE CREATED.

_____

_____

_____

_____

_____

_____

_____

BUY MODELING CLAY.

DAY 83

THE SINGULAR IMAGE
IS WHAT HAUNTS US
AND BECOMES ART.

_____

_____

_____

_____

_____

_____

WATCH A SQUIRREL.

DAY 84

eARly CAVe Paintings

MAKE A PAINTING IN SAND.

DAY 85

Later cave paintings

BUY WATERCOLORS.

DAY 86

SHADOW ARTISTS ARE GRAVITATING TO THEIR RIGHTFUL TRIBE BUT CANNOT YET CLAIM THEIR BIRTHRIGHT.

LISTEN TO GOSPEL MUSIC.

DAY 87

ARTISTS THEMSELVES, BUT
IGNORANT OF THEIR TRUE
IDENTITY, SHADOW ARTISTS
ARE TO BE FOUND SHADOWING
DECLARED ARTISTS.

_____
_____
_____
_____
_____
_____
_____

DRESS AS A LITERARY CHARACTER.

DAY 88

Is this what she means about being a shadow artist?

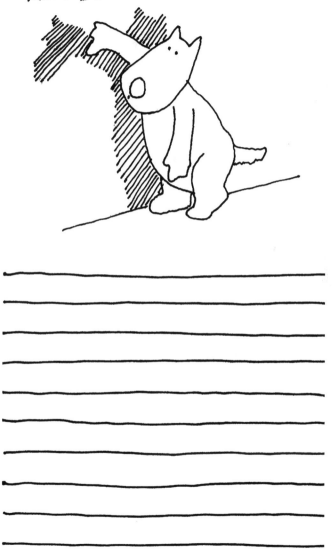

TRACE A FRIEND'S SILHOUETTE.

DAY 89

WE BECOME SHADOW ARTISTS
BECAUSE WE HAVE BEEN
FRIGHTENED OR DISCOURAGED.

_____

_____

_____

_____

_____

_____

_____

BUILD A FORT WITH BLANKETS.

DAY 90

DRAW ON FRECKLES.

DAY 91

LIST 3 old enemies OF
YOUR CREATIVE SELF.
Yes, Sister ANNA FROM
5TH GRADE does COUNT.

VISIT AN OLDIES BUT GOLDIES RECORD SHOP.

DAY 92

UNFORTUNATELY, MANY OF US HAVE WET BLANKET MOMMIES— AND A WHOLE ARMY OF WET BLANKET SURROGATE MOMMIES—THOSE FRIENDS WHO HAVE OUR SECOND, THIRD, AND FOURTH THOUGHTS FOR US. THE TRICK IS NOT TO LET THEM BE THAT WAY.

LIST 3 OF YOUR CREATIVE CHAMPIONS.

DAY 93

A PERFECTIONIST FRIEND CAN DAMPEN THE ARDOR OF A YOUNG ARTIST WHO IS JUST LEARNING TO LET IT RIP.

LIST 5 THINGS THAT MAKE YOU MAD.

DAY 94

BLOCKING
BOGEYMEN ARE BIG SCARY
MONSTERS TO YOUR ARTIST.

_____
_____
_____
_____
_____
_____
_____
_____
_____

BUY FUN GLOVES.

DAY 95

1ST MUSIC TEACHER

F

YOUR
MONSTER
HALL
OF
FAME

WRITE A PRAYER.

DAY 96

DO NOT INDULGE—

_____
_____
_____
_____
_____
_____
_____

ILLUSTRATE YOUR PRAYER.

DAY 97

OR TOLERATE ANYONE WHO THROWS COLD WATER IN YOUR DIRECTION.

BUY A GOLDFISH.

IF SOMEONE SERVES YOU A WET BLANKET CHOOSE SOMETHING ELSE FROM THE MENU.

MAKE HUMMUS.

DAY 99

LIST THREE NURTURING FRIENDS. WHICH OF THEIR TRAITS SERVE YOU PARTICULARLY WELL?

_____

_____

_____

_____

_____

_____

_____

_____

MAKE UP A SONG.

DAY 100

BE ALERT FOR SUPPORT
AND ENCOURAGEMENT
FROM UNEXPECTED
QUARTERS.

_____

_____

_____

_____

_____

_____

SING TO A FRIEND.

DAY 101

GO TO A JEWELER'S.

DAY 102

WHICH FRIENDS NURTURE YOU AND YOUR EXPERIMENTS— FASHION OR OTHERWISE?

_____
_____
_____
_____
_____
_____
_____
_____
_____
_____

MAKE A MASK FROM A BROWN PAPER BAG.

DAY 103

CREATIVITY GROWS
AMONG FRIENDS.

_____

_____

_____

_____

_____

_____

MAKE A BOOK OF QUOTES
FROM YOUR FRIENDS

DAY 104

ONE OF OUR CHIEF NEEDS AS CREATIVE BEINGS IS SUPPORT.

_____

_____

_____

_____

_____

_____

_____

_____

LOOK AT YOUR OLD PHOTO ALBUMS.

DAY 105

USE
LOVE
FOR
YOUR
ARTIST
TO
CURE
ITS
FEAR.

LIE STILL IN THE SUN FOR 10 MINUTES.

DAY 106

MY ARTIST IS A CHILD.

THE NATURAL CHILD WITHIN.

GO TO A TOY STORE.

DAY 107

SPENDING TIME IN SOLITUDE
WITH YOUR ARTIST CHILD IS
ESSENTIAL TO SELF-NURTURING.

_____

_____

_____

_____

_____

_____

COLOR IN A COLORING BOOK.

DAY 108

ART REQUIRES A SAFE HATCHERY—
WE LEARN TO PROTECT OUR ARTIST
CHILD FROM SHAME.

BUY A SQUIRT GUN.

DAY 109

REMEMBER, YOUR ARTIST IS A CHILD. FIND AND PROTECT THAT CHILD.

Go CAMPING.

DAY 110

OUR ARTIST IS ACTUALLY OUR INNER
PLAYMATE. AS WITH ALL PLAYMATES
IT IS JOY, NOT DUTY, THAT MAKES
FOR A LASTING BOND.

MEET A PARAKEET.

DAY 111

IF WE HAVE LISTENED TO OUR ARTIST CHILD WITHIN, IT HAS BEGUN TO FEEL MORE AND MORE SAFE.

_____

_____

_____

_____

_____

_____

TAKE A JAZZ IMPROVISATION LESSON.

DAY 112

WE CAN LEARN TO COMFORT
OUR ARTIST CHILD OVER
UNFAIR CRITICISM.

MAKE ICE CREAM.

DAY 113

ARE YOU CODDLING YOUR ARTIST
CHILD WITH CHILDHOOD LOVES?

_____

_____

_____

_____

_____

_____

_____

_____

_____

MAKE A COLORING BOOK.

DAY 114

AS A CREATIVE BEING, YOU WILL BE MORE PRODUCTIVE WHEN COAXED THAN WHEN BULLIED.

BUY GLITTERY STICKERS FOR YOUR CHECKBOOK

DAY 115

WHAT IS THE PAYOFF IN
KEEPING YOUR DESTRUCTIVE
FRIENDS?

_____

_____

_____

_____

_____

_____

DAY 116

DO NOT EXPECT YOUR BLOCKED FRIENDS TO APPLAUD YOUR RECOVERY.

_____

_____

_____

_____

_____

_____

_____

WRITE A SINGLES AD FOR YOURSELF.

DAY 117

A PRODUCTIVE ARTIST IS QUITE OFTEN A HAPPY PERSON. THIS CAN BE VERY THREATENING TO THOSE WHO ARE USED TO GETTING THEIR NEEDS MET BY BEING UNHAPPY.

LIST 10 HILARIOUS MOMENTS.

DAY 118

SELF-APPOINTED HOITY TOITIES

God FORBID THE INTELLECTUALS SHOULD LAUGH AT US.

MAYBE THEY NEED A GOOD LAUGH...

_____
_____
_____
_____
_____
_____
_____

MAKE UP A JOKE.

DAY 119

Go ROLLERBLADING.

DAY 120

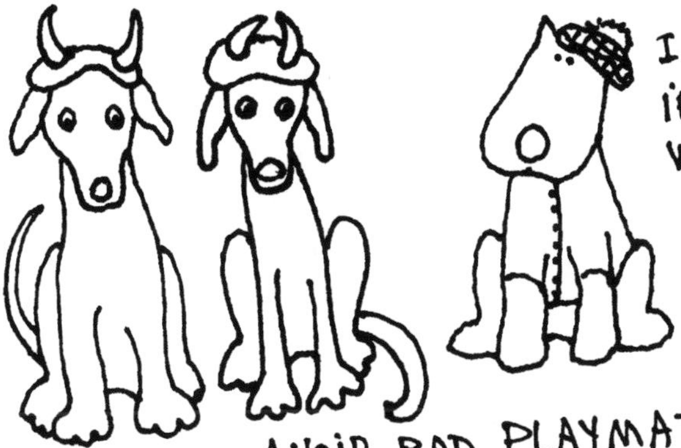

AVOID BAD PLAYMATES

MAKE A STUFFED ANIMAL.

DAY 121

THE MOST POISONOUS PLAYMATES
FOR US ARE THOSE WHOSE OWN
CREATIVITY IS STILL BLOCKED.

_____

_____

_____

_____

_____

_____

WALK A DOG.

DAY 122

CRAZYMAKERS CAN TAKE OVER YOUR WHOLE LiFE.

THEY ARE POiSONOUS FOR ANY SUSTAINED CREATiVE WORK.

GO FLY A KiTE.

DAY 123

CRAZYMAKERS LIKE DRAMA.

FIND A NEW INCENSE HOLDER.

DAY 124

CRAZYMAKERS ARE
LONG ON PROBLEMS,
SHORT ON SOLUTIONS.

BUY INCENSE.

DAY 125

CRAZYMAKERS CREATE
STORM CENTERS.
THEY SAP YOUR
CREATIVITY...

_____
_____
_____
_____
_____
_____

MAKE HOMEMADE SOUP.

DAY 126

CRAZYMAKERS
CARE ABOUT NOBODY ELSE'S
SCHEDULE BUT THEIR OWN.

DECORATE YOUR PET'S DINNER DISH.

DAY 127

IF I AllOW MYSELF TO BE BULLIED AND COWED BY OTHER PEOPLE'S URGES FOR ME TO BE MORE NORMAL OR MORE NICE, I SEll MYSELF OUT.

_____

_____

_____

_____

_____

_____

_____

PAINT YOUR KITCHEN RED.

DAY 128

DRAW A SACRED CIRCLE AROUND YOUR RECOVERY.

VISIT SOME HIGH PLACES.

DAY 129

THE BLOCKED ARTIST SPENDS ENERGY ON SELF-HATRED, REGRET, JEALOUSY, GRIEF AND SELF-DOUBT.

MAKE CURTAINS.

DAY 130

CREATIVITY IS OXYGEN FOR OUR SOULS.

BUY A DIME-STORE WIG.

DAY 131

ARTIST BRAIN IS OUR
INVENTOR, OUR VERY
OWN PERSONAL
ABSENT-MINDED
PROFESSOR.

COLLECT BEAUTIFUL LEAVES.

DAY 132

LIFE IS
ENERGY.
PURE
CREATIVE
ENERGY.

FIND A PRETTY ROCK.

DAY 133

THERE IS AN
UNDERLYING,
IN-DWELLING
CREATIVE
FORCE
INFUSING
ALL OF
LIFE —

INCLUDING
OURSELVES.

DRAW YOURSELF.

DAY 134

CREATIVITY IS OUR TRUE NATURE.

_____
_____
_____
_____
_____
_____
_____
_____

BAKE COOKIES.

DAY 135

IN A SENSE, AS WE ARE
CREATIVE BEINGS, OUR
LIVES BECOME OUR WORK OF ART.

_____

_____

_____

_____

_____

_____

PAINT YOUR BEDROOM WALL.

DAY 136

AS GRAY, AS CONTROlLED, AS DREAM-
LESS AS WE MAY STRIVE TO BE,
THE FIRE
OF OUR
DREAMS
WilL NOT
STAY
BURiED.

LIST 50 THINGS YOU ARE PROUD OF.

DAY 137

WIPE THE MIRROR -
YOUR IMAGE
MAY
SURPRISE
YOU...

GET COLORED CONTACTS.

DAY 138

AS A KID, I DREAMED OF BEING...

_____
_____
_____
_____
_____
_____
_____
_____

COLLAGE A SELF-PORTRAIT.

DAY 139

MY FAVORITE CHILDHOOD
GAME WAS...

_____

_____

_____

_____

_____

_____

_____

_____

MAKE A PIÑATA.

DAY 140

MY FAVORITE
CHILDHOOD
TOY WAS...

_____

_____

_____

_____

_____

_____

_____

_____

MAKE A PUPPET.

DAY 141

AS A KiD, I MISSED THE CHANCE TO...

GO TO THE CIRCUS.

DAY 142

AS A KID,
I NEEDED
MORE...

_____
_____
_____
_____
_____
_____
_____

VISIT A PUPPY.

DAY 143

THE IDEAL IS TO RE-COVER THE
DISTANCE WE HAVE DRIFTED
FROM OUR AUTHENTIC
CREATIVE SELVES...

_____
_____
_____
_____
_____

WRITE A LETTER FROM YOUR
8-YEAR-OLD SELF TO YOU.

DAY 144

AS A KID, I WISHED FOR MY VERY OWN...

GET ANOTHER PARAKEET.

DAY 145

PET A CAT.

DAY 146

MANY OF US WISH WE WERE MORE CREATIVE. OUR LIVES FEEL SOMEHOW FLAT.

MAKE PAPER DOLLS.

DAY 147

ALTHOUGH WE SELDOM CONNECT THE DOTS, MANY OF OUR PRESENT-DAY LOSSES ARE CONNECTED TO OUR EARLIER CONDITIONING.

DRAW A CHILDREN'S STORY.

DAY 148

THOSE OF US WHO GET BOGGED DOWN BY FEAR BEFORE ACTION ARE USUALLY BEING SABOTAGED BY AN OLDER ENEMY, SHAME.

WRITE A LETTER FROM YOUR 80-YEAR-OLD SELF TO YOU.

DAY 149

IF I HAD HAD A PERFECT CHILDHOOD, I'D HAVE GROWN UP TO BE...

_____

_____
_____
_____
_____
_____
_____
_____

GO TO THE PARK AND WRITE A LETTER.

DAY 150

ANGER IS OUR FRIEND.
NOT A NICE FRIEND, NOT A
GENTLE FRIEND. BUT A VERY,
VERY LOYAL FRIEND.

_____

_____

_____

_____

_____

WEAR ALL BLACK.

DAY 151

CLARITY IS A FRUIT OF THE MORNING PAGES.

GO LOOK AT GEMSTONES.

DAY 152

WE KNOW WHAT'S
BOTHERING US AND WHY.

_____
_____
_____
_____
_____
_____
_____

DO A PUZZLE.

DAY 153

GO BOWLING.

DAY 154

TAKE PICTURES OF YOUR FEET.

DAY 155

MAKE A PILLOW.

DAY 156

IF MORNING PAGES WASH YOUR BRAIN, DOES IT SHRINK?

MAKE SEASHELL ORNAMENTS.

DAY 157

TAKE A TANGO LESSON.

DAY 158

THE FLOW MAY FEEL SO
STRONG THAT YOU WILL
NEED THE MORNING PAGES
TO TRAVEL COMFORTABLY
IN ITS CELERITY.

WRITE A NURSERY RHYME.

DAY 159

I HAVE LEARNED, AS A
RULE OF THUMB, NEVER TO
ASK WHETHER YOU CAN DO
SOMETHING. SAY INSTEAD
THAT YOU ARE DOING IT.
THEN FASTEN YOUR SEAT
BELT. THE MOST REMARK-
ABLE THINGS FOLLOW.

DECORATE A BACKPACK.

DAY 160

TAKE A SMALL STEP IN THE DIRECTION OF A DREAM AND WATCH THE SYNCHRONOUS DOORS FLYING OPEN.

GO PEOPLE-WATCHING DOWNTOWN.

DAY 161

KNOCK AND IT SHALL
BE OPENED TO YOU.

_____

_____

_____

_____

_____

PREPARE A SCAVENGER HUNT.

DAY 162

Did you experience any synchronicity this week?

_____

_____

_____

_____

_____

_____

DECORATE YOUR DATEBOOK.

DAY 163

WE CAN LEARN NOT ONLY TO LISTEN BUT ALSO TO HEAR WITH INCREAS-ING ACCURACY THAT INSPIRED INTUITIVE VOICE THAT SAYS, "DO THIS, TRY THIS, SAY THIS."

GO TO AN OUTDOOR CONCERT.

DAY 164

SCULPTING Buddha

MAKE SOMETHING OUT OF CLAY.

DAY 165

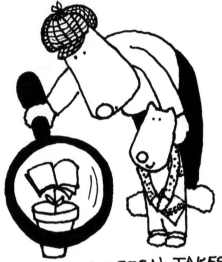

IT OFTEN TAKES
ANOTHER ARTIST TO SEE
THE EMBRYONIC WORK
THAT IS TRYING
TO SPROUT.

TRY ON NEW EYEGLASSES.

DAY 166

WE CAN LEARN NOT TO DENY
AND STUFF OUR FEELINGS
WHEN WE HAVE BEEN
ARTISTICALLY SAVAGED.

MAKE EASTER EGGS.

DAY 167

DON'T PLAY IN THE MUD AND EAT WORMS.

GO TO A MOVIE.

DAY 168

GeT BACK ON THE HORSE.
MAKE AN iMMEDiATE
COMMiTMENT TO DO
SOMETHiNG CREATiVE.

NAME YOUR HOUSE.

DAY 169

Do it. Creativity
is the only cure
for criticism.

_____

_____

_____

_____

_____

_____

MAKE A GINGERBREAD HOUSE.

IT IS THIS Willingness TO ONCE MORE BE A BEGINNER THAT DISTINGUISHES A CREATIVE CAREER.

EXPERIMENT WITH PASTELS.

DAY 171

The Terror of Being Bad is often All
That stands in the way of our being good

DRAW YOUR PET.

DAY 172

THE NEED TO PRODUCE A GREAT WORK OF ART MAKES IT HARD TO PRODUCE ANY ART AT ALL.

DO NEEDLEPOINT.

DAY 173

TO THE PERFECTIONIST
THERE IS ALWAYS ROOM FOR
IMPROVEMENT. THE PERFEC-
TIONIST CALLS THIS HUMILITY.
IN REALITY, IT IS EGOTISM.

_____

_____

_____

_____

_____

_____

MAKE FUDGE.

DAY 174

DONATE YOUR TIME TO THE ASPCA.

ONCE WE ARE WILLING TO ACCEPT THAT ANYTHING WORTH DOING MIGHT EVEN BE WORTH DOING BADLY, OUR OPTIONS WIDEN.

PLAY A HARMONICA.

GILD PINECONES.

DAY 177

SOMETIMES I WIll WRITE BADLY, DRAW BADLY, PAINT BADLY, PERFORM BADLY. I HAVE A RIGHT TO DO THAT TO GET TO THE OTHER SIDE.

SING A FOLK SONG.

DAY 178

WE DENY THAT IN ORDER TO DO SOMETHING WEll WE MUST FIRST BE WilliNG TO DO IT BADLY.

BUY COLORED PENCILS.

DAY 179

USUALLY, WHEN WE SAY WE CAN'T DO SOMETHING, WHAT WE MEAN IS THAT WE WON'T DO SOMETHING UNLESS WE CAN GUARANTEE THAT WE'll DO IT PERFECTLY.

PAINT A FLOWERPOT.

DAY 180

IF I DIDN'T HAVE TO DO IT PERFECTLY, I WOULD TRY...

TREE BALLET.

CHASE A SQUIRREL.

DAY 181

DRAW A STICK HOUSE.

DAY 182

emember, it is in THE CRiDUCKS' JOB
description TO MAKE puddles. THEY LiKE puddles.

_____
_____
_____
_____
_____
_____
_____
_____
_____
_____

SIGN UP FOR SWIMMING LESSONS.

DAY 183

CRIDUCKS ASSUME
THEIR PROPER SIZE
WHEN WE'RE ON
OUR FEET.

POLISH YOUR BOOTS.

DAY 184

ARTIST
WARRIOR

MAKE A DOLL OF YOUR INTIMATE OTHER.

DAY 185

ARTISTS AND INTELLECTUALS
ARE NOT THE SAME ANIMAL.

LISTEN TO ROCK AND ROLL.

DAY 186

WHAT IF CRITICS HATE IT?

_____

_____

_____

_____

_____

_____

_____

_____

_____

_____

_____

WRITE A SONG FOR CHILDREN.

DAY 187

SPEED
KILLS
THE
CENSOR.

TRY A SKATEBOARD.

DAY 188

AS WE GAIN STRENGTH, SO WILL SOME OF THE ATTACKS OF SELF-DOUBT.

YOU'RE TOO OLD

YOU LOOK SILLY

YOU NEED A REAL JOB

SIT ON A MOTORCYCLE.

DAY 189

BE FIRM WITH YOURSELF AND
DON'T PICK UP THAT FIRST DOUBT.

DAY 190

THEO
AND THE
HOTTEST
DOGS

WE All LIKE CREDIT WHERE
CREDIT IS DUE. AS ARTISTS,
WE DON'T AlWAYS GET IT.

PHOTOGRAPH YOUR WORK DAY.

DAY 191

COMMERCIAL WORK REQUIRES
NEGOTIATING SKILLS

MAKE A PUPPET THEATER.

DAY 192

ANY ORIGINAL THOUGHT CAN LOOK
PRETTY DANGEROUS TO OUR CENSOR.

Go LOOK AT COWS.

DAY 193

SEND A POSTCARD TO YOURSELF THAT SAYS, "YOU ARE DOING GREAT..."

Go TO A STATIONERY STORE.

DAY 194

RECOVERY URGES REEXAMINING OUR DEFINITIONS OF CREATIVITY AND EXPANDING THEM TO INCLUDE WHAT IN THE PAST WE CALLED HOBBIES.

LEARN ORIGAMI.

DAY 195

LIST TEN
FORBIDDEN
JOYS—

THINGS YOU'D LOVE TO DO OR HAVE
BUT AREN'T "Allowed" TO DO OR HAVE.

GET A CHOCOLATE CROISSANT.

DAY 196

PICTURE
YOUR
IDEAL
DAY.
Allow YOURSELF TO BE AND TO
HAVE YOUR HEART'S DESIRES.

_____
_____
_____
_____
_____
_____
_____
_____
_____
_____
_____

TRY ON WIGS.

DAY 197

EXPERIMENT WITH SOLITUDE.

_____

_____

_____

_____

_____

_____

_____

_____

_____

MAKE A GARDEN.

DAY 198

HAPPINESS TOUCHSTONES:
MAKE A QUICK LIST OF
THINGS YOU LOVE. POST
IT AS A REMINDER.

CHOPIN
SOUP
CHICORY
SPARKLY TOY
RIVER ROCKS
VELVET
CATS

GET NEW P.J.'s.

DAY 199

WRITE A LETTER FROM YOU AT EIGHTY TO YOU AT YOUR CURRENT AGE. WHAT WOULD YOU TEII YOURSELF?

DESIGN STATIONERY.

DAY 200

CHOOSE AN ARTIST TOTEM.

IT MIGHT BE A Doll.

_____

_____

_____

_____

_____

_____

_____

_____

_____

MAKE PUPPETS OF YOU AND
YOUR SIGNIFICANT OTHER.

DAY 201

IF YOU FEEL STUCK IN YOUR LIFE OR IN YOUR ART, FEW JUMP STARTS ARE MORE EFFECTIVE THAN A WEEK OF READING DEPRIVATION.

SEW AN APRON.

DAY 202

Swing!

SING A CHRISTMAS CAROL.

DAY 203

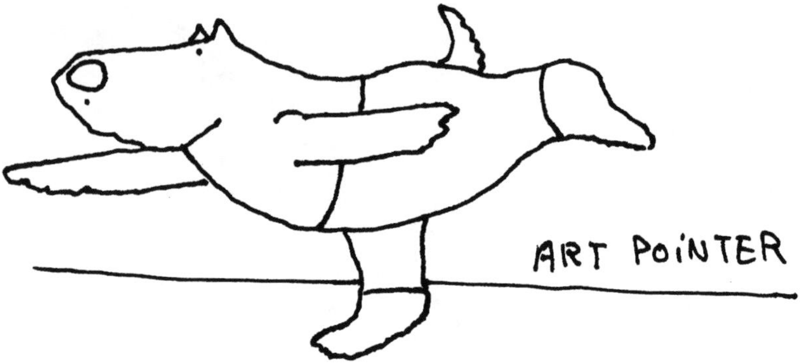

ART POINTER

GO TO A MUSEUM.

DAY 204

MAYBE THAT'S WHERE
HE KEPT HIS SKETCHBOOK...

BUY NICE PENCILS.

DAY 205

ART MATURES SPASMODICAIIY AND
REQUIRES UGLY DUCKLING GROWTH
STAGES.

_____

_____

_____

_____

_____

_____

_____

MAKE BREAD.

DAY 206

AS WE WITHDRAW AND ARTICULATE OUR OWN GOALS, OUR PERSONAL FLEXIBILITY INCREASES, WHILE OUR MALLEABILITY TO OTHERS' WHIMS DECREASES.

_____
_____
_____
_____
_____
_____
_____
_____

TAKE A YOGA CLASS.

DAY 207

MANY OF US FIND THAT WE HAVE SQUANDERED OUR OWN CREATIVE ENERGIES BY INVESTING DISPROPORTIONATELY IN THE LIVES, HOPES, DREAMS AND PLANS OF OTHERS.

WE'RE BROKE

GO SWIMMING.

DAY 208

SOUP AND
POPCORN dinners
MAY GIVE YOU MORE
TIME TO CREATE, BUT
YOU WON'T LIVE AS LONG TO DO IT!
FEED YOUR ARTIST MORE GOOD THINGS.

TRY NEW VEGETABLES.

DAY 209

GO TO CHINATOWN.

DAY 210

WHEN WE CAN'T GET OTHERS TO LEAVE US ALONE, WE EVENTUALLY ABANDON OURSELVES.

WHAT'S LEFT IS A SHELL OF OUR WHOLE SELF. LIKE A LISTLESS CIRCUS ANIMAL PRODDED INTO PERFORMING, IT DOES ITS TRICKS.

TRY ON BALL GOWNS.

DAY 211

MANY PEOPLE, CAUGHT IN THE VIRTUE TRAP, DO NOT APPEAR TO BE SELF DESTRUCTIVE TO THE CASUAL EYE.

PUT A HYACINTH BY YOUR BED.

DAY 212

DRAW A CARTOON.

DAY 213

MAKE A COLLAGE.

DAY 214

THE VIRTUE TRAP—

WE HAVE EMBRACED A LONG-SUFFERING ARTISTIC ANOREXIA AS A MARTYR'S CROSS.

MAKE POPSICLES.

DAY 215

TEN WAYS I AM MEAN TO MYSELF:

NO MUSIC →

OLD GLASSES

POPCORN DINNER

HANDME DOWNS

OLD CANVAS

BROKEN TV

FAT IS FREE

↑ NOT CALLING FRIENDS

← TOO TIGHT

← HOUSE GUESTS

GO TO THE ZOO.

GO TO A FISH STORE.

DAY 217

THEATRE OF THEO

IF I DON'T CREATE
I GET CRABBY.

_____

_____

_____

_____

_____

_____

_____

MAKE AND DECORATE CUT OUT COOKIES.

DAY 218

WHO: I AM JEALOUS OF THEO.
WHY: HE'S OUT HAVING FUN.
ACTION: BARK 'TIL THEY
        LET ME OUT.

ON PAPER, MAKE YOUR
JEALOUSY MAP. BE SPECIFIC.

BUILD A SNOWMAN.

DAY 219

GO TO A PLANETARIUM.

WHATEVER YOU THINK YOU CAN DO OR BELIEVE YOU CAN DO, BEGIN IT. ACTION HAS MAGIC, GRACE, AND POWER IN IT.

—Goethe

GO BUY A CRYSTAL.

DAY 221

LEAViNG tHE NeST
iS SCARY.

_____
_____
_____
_____
_____
_____
_____
_____

MAKE A BiRDHOUSE.

DAY 222

Leap + THE NET will APPEAR.

CALLIGRAPHY YOUR FAVORITE QUOTE.

DAY 223

Dance, and the WORLD Dances WiTH you.

_____
_____
_____
_____
_____
_____
_____
_____
_____
_____

TAKE A SINGING LESSON.

DAY 224

iF THE WORLD iS A STAGE, GO ON AND STRUT YOUR STUFF!

LEARN A SPANISH SONG.

DAY 225

Let Go.

_____
_____
_____
_____
_____
_____
_____
_____
_____

GO WINDOW SHOPPING.

DAY 226

CREATIVITY
REQUIRES
FAITH.
FAITH REQUIRES
THAT WE
RELINQUISH
CONTROL...

TURN A SOMERSAULT.

DAY 227

AS ARTISTS, WE TUNE
IN TO HEAR WHAT IS IN
OUR UNDERGROUND
RIVER — MORE LIKE
TAKING
DICTATION
THAN ANYTHING
FANCY HAVING
TO DO WITH
ART.

TAKE A SAUNA.

DAY 228

MYSTERY IS AT THE
HEART OF CREATIVITY.
THAT AND SURPRISE.
AS CREATIVE CHANNELS,

WE NEED TO TRUST THE DARKNESS.

WRITE A FAIRY TALE.

DAY 229

CREATIVE PROGRESS IS MADE BY LEAPS OF FAITH, SOME SMALL AND SOME LARGE.

BUY SHOELACES.

DAY 230

IN TRUTH, ARTISTS ARE PEOPLE WHO HAVE LEARNED TO LIVE WITH DOUBT AND DO THE WORK ANYWAY.

DOUBT

DOUBT IF SHE CAN DO IT!

MORE DOUBT

GO BAREFOOT.

DAY 231

GET SOME DAFFODILS.

DAY 232

A FOOL
MAY BE,
BUT A
TALENTED
FOOL.

PLAY DRESS-UP.

DAY 233

Go To A CHILDREN'S BOOKSTORE.

DAY 234

AS
WE
MOVE
TOWARD
OUR DREAMS,
WE MOVE TOWARD OUR DIVINITY.

VISIT A PLAYGROUND.

DAY 235

STOP TELLING YOURSELF THAT
YOUR DREAMS DON'T MATTER.

_____

_____

_____

_____

_____

_____

_____

_____

_____

STAY UP 'TiL SUNRISE.

DAY 236

LIFE IS WHAT WE MAKE OF IT.

CROSS-COUNTRY SKI.

DAY 237

VERY OFTEN A RISK IS WORTH TAKING SIMPLY FOR THE SAKE OF TAKING IT.

_____

_____

_____

_____

_____

_____

_____

TRY KABUKI MAKEUP.

DAY 238

WE'VE ALL HEARD THAT THE UNEXAMINED LIFE IS NOT WORTH LIVING, BUT CONSIDER TOO THAT THE UNLIVED LIFE IS NOT WORTH EXAMINING.

MAKE PARTY INVITATIONS.

DAY 239

WHEN WE DO WHAT WE ARE MEANT TO DO, MONEY COMES TO US, DOORS OPEN FOR US, WE FEEL USEFUL, AND THE WORK WE DO FEELS LIKE PLAY TO US.

MAKE A JEWELRY BOX.

DAY 240

ALTHOUGH MANY OF US DO
MAKE MONEY AT IT, CREATIVITY
IS ITS OWN REWARD.

_____

_____

_____

_____

_____

_____

DECORATE YOUR CALENDAR.

DAY 241

STOP WAITING UNTIL YOU
MAKE ENOUGH MONEY TO
DO SOMETHING YOU'd REALLY LOVE.

DESIGN A JEWELRY COLLECTION.

DAY 242

WE UNCONCIOUSLY SET A LIMIT ON HOW MUCH GOD CAN GIVE US OR HELP US.

Go TO AN ORIENTAL RUG STORE.

DAY 243

MAKE A PIE.

DAY 244

THE TRUTH IS THAT WE ARE MEANT
TO BE BOUNTIFUL AND LIVE.

_____

_____

_____

_____

_____

_____

_____

_____

GO TO THE BOTANICAL GARDENS.

DAY 245

WE ARE MISEALY BECAUSE WE
DON'T WANT OUR LUCK TO RUN OUT.

PLANT AN HERB GARDEN.

DAY 246

God HAS LOTS OF MONEY.

God HAS AN ENDLESS ABUNDANCE OF IDEAS, LOVE, JOBS, ETC., FOR US.

BUY SOCKS.

DAY 247

CAUTION: ROSE-
COLORED GLASSES
MAY NOT OBSCURE
VISION...

PLANT SOME BULBS.

DAY 248

I BEGAN TO NOTICE THAT EACH
MOMENT WAS NOT WITHOUT
ITS BEAUTY.

_____

_____

_____

_____

_____

_____

VISIT A PLANT STORE.

DAY 249

BECAUSE MANY OF US UNCONCIOUSLY HARBOR THE FEARFUL BELIEF THAT God WOULD FIND OUR CREATIONS DECADENT OR FRIVOLOUS OR WORSE, WE TEND TO DISCOUNT THIS CREATOR-TO-CREATOR HELP.

_____

_____

_____

_____

_____

PICK APPLES.

DAY 250

ALTHOUGH JUNG'S PAPER ON SYNCHRONIC-
ITY WAS A CORNERSTONE OF HIS THOUGHT,
EVEN MANY JUNGIANS PREFER TO BELIEVE
IT WAS SORT OF A SIDE ISSUE.
JUNG MIGHT DIFFER WITH THEM.

GO TO A FLEA MARKET.

DAY 251

Balloons: TOO GOOD TO BE TRUE / IT WAS JUST LUCK / ITS TOO WEIRD / I DOUBT IT / IT'S JUST A COINCIDENCE

WE HAVE OUR DOUBTS ABOUT ALL OF THIS CREATOR/CREATIVITY STUFF, AND THOSE DOUBTS ARE VERY POWERFUL. UNLESS WE AIR THEM, THEY CAN SABOTAGE US.

SKEPTIC

BUY A RUBBER STAMP AND GREAT INK.

DAY 252

BY TRUSTING, WE LEARN TO TRUST.

_____

_____

_____

_____

_____

_____

_____

_____

TRACE YOUR HANDS.

DAY 253

EXPECT THE UNIVERSE TO
SUPPORT YOUR DREAM. IT Will.

MAKE A CHRISTMAS PRESENT.

DAY 254

VISIT A POSTER STORE.

DAY 255

WE ARE ASKED TO EXPAND IN ORDER THAT WE NOT CONTRACT.

_____

_____

_____

_____

_____

_____

TRY ON HATS.

DAY 256

ARTISTS LIKE
OTHER ARTISTS.

ORGANIZE A CLOTHING SWAP.

DAY 257

FOR ARTISTS—
AS WITH A
GARDEN—
THERE IS
NO ONE
FLOWER
THAT
CANCELS
THE NEED
FOR ANOTHER.

BUY TULIPS.

DAY 258

STOP TELLING YOURSELF THAT DREAMS DON'T MATTER, THAT THEY ARE ONLY DREAMS AND THAT YOU SHOULD BE MORE SENSIBLE.

BUY STICK-ON STARS.

DAY 259

WE ARE MEANT TO MIDWIFE
DREAMS FOR ONE ANOTHER
IN A SACRED CIRCLE.

_____

_____

_____

_____

_____

_____

_____

_____

BAKE A PIE AND GIVE IT TO A FRIEND

DAY 260

COMPETITION LIES AT THE ROOT OF MUCH CREATIVE BLOCKAGE.

MAKE PLACEMATS.

DAY 261

PLAN A BIRTHDAY PARTY.

DAY 262

ONLY WHEN WE ARE BEING JOYFULLY CREATIVE CAN WE RELEASE THE OBSESSION WITH OTHERS AND HOW THEY ARE DOING.

SKETCH A BUILDING.

DAY 263

THE FOOTRACE MENTALITY IS ALWAYS THE EGO'S DEMAND TO BE NOT JUST GOOD BUT ALSO FIRST AND BEST.

_____

_____

_____

_____

_____

_____

_____

MAKE CHRISTMAS ORNAMENTS.

DAY 264

WANTING MORE WILL ALWAYS SNAP AT OUR HEELS, DISCREDIT OUR ACCOMPLISHMENTS, ERODE OUR JOY AT ANOTHER'S ACCOMPLISHMENT.

BUY A DISPOSABLE CAMERA.

DAY 265

JEALOUSY IS ALWAYS
A MASK FOR FEAR.

PHOTOGRAPH FLOWERS CLOSE UP.

DAY 266

HAVING THE
BIGGEST
PUMPKIN
ISN'T
ALWAYS
THE
BEST
FOR
YOU.

REPOT A PLANT.

DAY 267

FAME MEANS GETTING TO PISS
IN All THE RIGHT PLACES.

_____
_____
_____
_____
_____
_____
_____
_____

GO TO A DOG SHOW.

DAY 268

THERE IS NEVER ENOUGH OF THE FAME DRUG.

_____

_____

_____

_____

_____

_____

_____

WRITE TO AN OLD TEACHER.

DAY 269

FAME IS NOT THE SAME AS
SUCCESS...

FAME IS REALLY A SUBSTITUTE
FOR SELF-APPROVAL.

_____

_____

_____

_____

_____

_____

_____

MAKE A SIGN FOR YOUR ROOM.

DAY 270

LUXURY IS VERY IMPORTANT.

WE NEED TO PAMPER OUR ARTIST.

ROSES 2.4.1$

GET CHINESE DISHES.

DAY 271

WORK ABUSE CREATES IN OUR ARTIST A CINDERELLA COMPLEX. WE ARE ALWAYS DREAMING OF THE BALL AND ALWAYS EXPERIENCING THE BALL AND CHAIN.

Go to a five and dime store.

DAY 272

IF I'M BESIDE
MYSELF WITH
WORRY, NEITHER
OF US CAN WORK.

DO A FINGER PAINTING.

DAY 273

MUST WE
LOOK All
GIFT HORSES
IN THE MOUTH?

_____
_____
_____
_____
_____
_____
_____
_____
_____
_____

VISIT A SADDLE SHOP.

DAY 274

IF I BECOME SOLVENT I'll MISS MY FAMILIAR PARAMETERS!

FEAR

POVERTY

DESIGN YOUR IDEAL HOME.

DAY 275

WE'RE NOT ACCUSTOMED TO THINKING THAT GOD'S WILL FOR US AND OUR OWN INNER DREAMS CAN COINCIDE.

BUY A NEW BROOM AND DECORATE IT WITH SPARKLES.

DAY 276

IT'S TOO
WEIRD
TO
IMAGINE
AN UNSEEN
HELPING
HAND?

GET A TAROT READING.

DAY 277

I OFTEN SENSE A SPIRITUAL ELECTRICITY I HAVE COME TO RELY ON IN TRANSCENDING MY OWN LIMITATIONS.

DRAW A CHAIR.

DAY 278

iF I HAD FAITH, I'd...

_____
_____
_____
_____
_____
_____
_____

MAKE A CANDLE HOLDER.

DAY 279

THE RIDE IS
SMOOTH IF
YOU DON'T
LOOK DOWN.

MAKE A KITE.

DAY 280

MOST OF THE TIME
WHEN WE ARE BLOCKED
IN AN AREA OF OUR LIFE
IT IS BECAUSE WE FEEL
SAFER THAT WAY.

MAKE A CASSEROLE.

DAY 281

QUESTION: DO YOU KNOW HOW OLD I'll BE BY THE TIME I LEARN TO PLAY THE PIANO?
ANSWER: SAME AGE YOU WOULD BE IF YOU DON'T.

GO TO A MUSIC STORE.

DAY 282

going for the high notes

BUY BELLS.

DAY 283

THE MUSIC IS
BIGGER THAN
WE ARE.

READ ALL NIGHT.

WRITE A HAIKU.

DAY 285

UNTIL WE KNOW BETTER, WE CALL A GREAT MANY CREATIVE SWANS UGLY DUCKLINGS.

TRY A NEW PERFUME.

DAY 286

ART
is
A
CATCH-
AND-
RELEASE
PROCESS.

GET A BIRD FEEDER.

DAY 287

IT IS IMPORTANT TO REMEMBER
THAT AT FIRST FLUSH, GOING
SANE FEELS EXACTLY LIKE
GOING CRAZY.

_____

_____

_____

_____

_____

_____

_____

_____

BUY MARBLES.

DAY 288

IT IS QUITE POSSIBLE TO
BE AN ARTIST AND
FINANCIALLY SUCCESSFUL.

_____
_____
_____
_____
_____
_____
_____
_____
_____

BUY PRETTY STAMPS.

DAY 289

RULE #1:
SHOW UP FOR YOUR ART.

_____

MAKE A MOBILE.

DAY 290

CREATIVITY LIES
NOT IN THE DONE
BUT IN DOING.

MAKE A STRING SCULPTURE.

DAY 291

STOP TELLING YOURSELF,
"IT'S TOO LATE."

MAKE MISO SOUP.

DAY 292

IF IT WEREN'T
TOO LATE, I'd...

EMBROIDER A PAIR OF JEANS.

DAY 293

DO NOT
CALL THE
INABILITY
TO START
LAZINESS.
CALL IT FEAR.

PLANT A TREE.

DAY 294

MAKING ART BEGINS WITH MAKING
HAY WHILE THE SUN SHINES.

_____

_____

_____

_____

_____

_____

_____

_____

CARVE A LITTLE PIECE OF WOOD.

DAY 295

WHERE DOES _YOUR_ TIME GO?

_____

_____

_____

_____

_____

_____

GET A GREAT VACUUM CLEANER.

DAY 296

Go WITH THE CREATIVE FLOW.

_____
_____
_____
_____
_____
_____
_____
_____
_____
_____
_____
_____
_____

COLLECT SEASHELLS.

DAY 297

_____
_____
_____
_____
_____
_____
_____

YEAH!
You Go!!

_____
_____
_____
_____
_____
_____
_____
_____
_____

DECORATE A CAKE.

DAY 298

WALK IN THE WOODS.

DAY 299

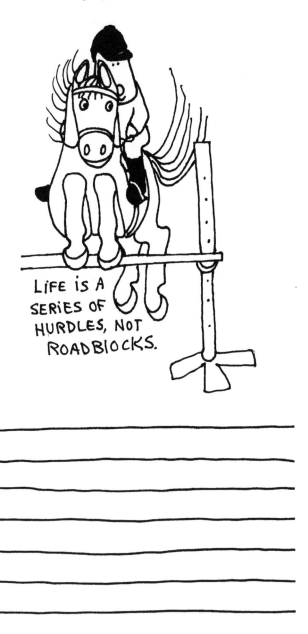

LIFE IS A SERIES OF HURDLES, NOT ROADBLOCKS.

VISIT AN AUTO SHOWROOM.

DAY 300

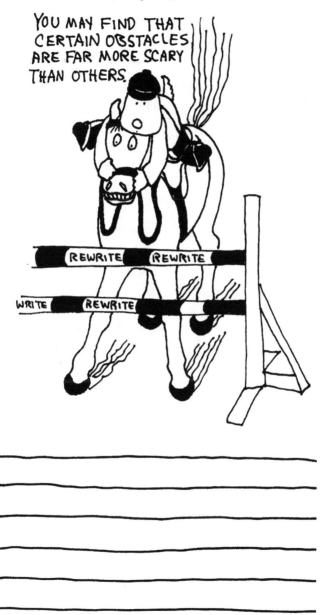

WALK BY WATER.

DAY 301

DECORATE A SWEATSHIRT.

DAY 302

WE COME UP TO A CREATIVE
JUMP, RUN OUT FROM IT LIKE
A SKITTISH HORSE, THEN
CIRCLE THE FIELD A FEW
TIMES BEFORE TRYING THE
FENCE AGAIN.

_____
_____
_____
_____
_____
_____
_____
_____

MEND   YOUR   SOCKS.

DAY 303

A SUCCESSFUL CREATIVE CAREER
IS ALWAYS BUILT ON
SUCCESSFUL
CREATIVE
FAILURES.

THE TRICK IS TO SURVIVE THEM.

_____
_____
_____
_____
_____
_____
_____
_____
_____
_____

PAINT YOUR BATHROOM.

DAY 304

TAKE CARE OF
YOURSELF.

_____

_____

_____

_____

_____

_____

_____

_____

_____

_____

_____

MAKE HOT COCOA.

DAY 305

Sometimes CAREER MOMENTUM Carries US.

MAKE A SWING.

DAY 306

WE USUALLY COMMIT CREATIVE
HARA-KIRI EITHER ON THE EVE
OF OR IN THE WAKE OF A FIRST
CREATIVE VICTORY.

CHANGE YOUR HAIR.

DAY 307

THE TEST.

YEAH. THE TEST.
IT'S LIKE WHEN
YOU'RE All SET
TO MARRY THE
NICE GUY, THE ONE
WHO TREATS YOU RIGHT, AND
MR. POISON GETS WIND OF IT AND
PHONES YOU UP.

MAKE A WEAVING.

DAY 308

YOU'RE ALL SET TO LEAVE THE BAD JOB

SPAIN OR BUST

AND THE BOSS FROM HELL SUDDENLY GIVES YOU YOUR FIRST RAISE IN FIVE YEARS...
DON'T BE FOOLED. DON'T BE FOOLED.

_____

_____

_____

_____

_____

BUY A NEW THROW RUG.

DAY 309

REMEMBER YOU ARE NOT SO MUCH ENCOUNTERING THE SHADOW AS JUST BUYING IT A CUP OF COFFEE AND LETTING IT PUT ITS TWO CENTS' WORTH IN INSTEAD OF DARKENING YOUR ENTIRE DAY.

_____

_____

_____

_____

_____

_____

_____

HANG SOME CHRISTMAS LIGHTS.

DAY 310

ON 7 PAPER STRIPS WRITE 1 WORD: ALCOHOL, DRUGS, SEX, WORK, MONEY, FOOD, FAMILY/FRIENDS.

DRAW ONE OF THE FOLDED STRIPS OUT OF AN ENVELOPE AND WRITE 5 WAYS IT HAS NEGATIVELY IMPACTED YOUR LIFE. DRAW 7 TIMES.

THE DEADLIES.

COLLECT FLOWERS TO DRY.

DAY 311

CONSTANT DRAMA AND NEVER TAKING RESPONSIBILITY FOR YOURSELF GETS IN THE WAY OF YOUR ART.

LEARN TO KNIT.

DAY 312

ALL HAT AND NO CATTLE IS LIKE ALL TALK AND NO ART.

DECORATE A TRUNK.

DAY 313

MAKE A PICTURE OUT OF STONES.

DAY 314

THE ENEMY.

LIGHT A CANDLE.

DAY 315

REARRANGE YOUR HOUSE.

DAY 316

AS BLOCKED CREATIVES
WE ARE WILLING TO GO
TO ALMOST ANY LENGTHS
TO REMAIN BLOCKED.

_____

_____

_____

_____

_____

_____

PAINT A SILK SCARF.

DAY 317

Don't Let Friends SQUANDER YOUR TIME.

_____

_____

_____

_____

_____

_____

_____

_____

_____

_____

DECORATE A FRAME.

DAY 318

TEll THE TRUTH.
WHAT IS THE
PAYOFF IN
KEEPING
YOUR
ARTISTIC
BLOCKS?

CLEAN OUT YOUR MEDICINE CABINET.

DAY 319

IF I SABOTAGE MY ARTIST I MAY WEll EXPECT AN EATING BINGE, A SEX BINGE, A TEMPER BINGE.

DECORATE A VASE.

DAY 320

FOOD IS OFTEN USED TO BLOCK ENERGY AND CHANGE.

PAINT A CHAIR.

DAY 321

EATING INSTEAD
OF WRITING?

MAKE NAPKIN RINGS.

DAY 322

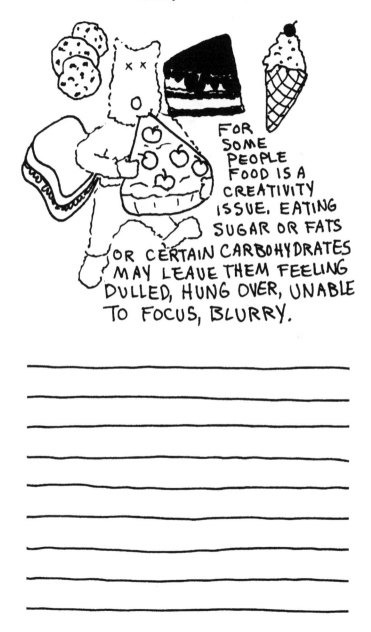

FOR SOME PEOPLE FOOD IS A CREATIVITY ISSUE. EATING SUGAR OR FATS OR CERTAIN CARBOHYDRATES MAY LEAVE THEM FEELING DULLED, HUNG OVER, UNABLE TO FOCUS, BLURRY.

PICK STRAWBERRIES.

DAY 323

SEX IS A GREAT CREATIVE BLOCK FOR MANY. HAS SEX OR LOVE OBSESSION BLOCKED MY CREATIVITY?

_____

_____

_____

_____

_____

_____

_____

_____

MAKE A VALENTINE FOR YOURSELF.

DAY 324

SET YOUR GOALS AND
SET YOUR BOUNDARIES.

_____
_____
_____
_____
_____
_____
_____

LIST YOUR INNER AND OUTER
CIRCLE OF FRIENDS

DAY 325

TO SHARE
OR NOT
TO
SHARE..
WHAT
A
QUESTION!

TREAT YOURSELF TO SUSHI ALONE.

DAY 326

IN DEALING WITH THE SUICIDE OF THE "NICE" SELF WE HAVE BEEN MAKING DO WITH, WE FIND A CERTAIN AMOUNT OF GRIEF TO BE ESSENTIAL.

BUY FANCY HANDKERCHIEFS.

DAY 327

How cute, Theo, are you playing dead ?!

No, I'm practicing to be a famous artist

_____
_____
_____
_____
_____
_____
_____
_____
_____
_____
_____
_____
_____

WEAR A COLOR THAT MEANS
SAFETY TO YOU

DAY 328

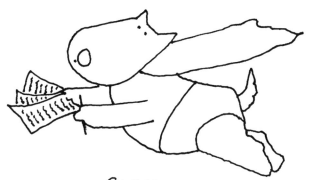

SUPER THEO
FLIES THROUGH
MORNING PAGES.

_____

_____

_____

_____

_____

_____

_____

_____

_____

_____

O TO THE LIBRARY AND LOOK AT ART BOOKS.

DAY 329

IN A CREATIVE LIFE, DROUGHTS ARE A NECESSITY. THE TIME IN THE DESERT BRINGS US CLARITY AND CHARITY.

_____

_____

_____

_____

_____

_____

_____

_____

MAKE LEMONADE.

DAY 330

A DROUGHT IS A TEARLESS TIME OF GRIEF. WE ARE BETWEEN DREAMS.

_____
_____
_____
_____
_____
_____
_____

BUY A CACTUS.

DAY 331

THE EXPERIENCE OF CREATIVE LIVING ARGUES THAT HOBBIES ARE IN FACT ESSENTIAL TO THE JOYFUL LIFE.

MAKE A PIECE OF FOLK ART.

DAY 332

I DON'T DO IT MUCH,
BUT I ENJOY...

BAKE A CAKE.

DAY 333

MEDITATING IN ANY
FORM IS GOOD FOR
YOUR CREATIVE SPIRIT.

PAINT A BOOKCASE.

DAY 334

scrubbing can help
contact our inner
compass. (so it's good
for something.)

_____

_____

_____

_____

_____

_____

_____

_____

_____

_____

_____

_____

DRIVE IN THE COUNTRY.

DAY 335

CLEARING: ANY NEW CHANGES
IN YOUR HOME ENVIRONMENT?
MAKE SOME.

_____
_____
_____
_____
_____
_____

BUY A NEW DISH TOWEL.

DAY 336

TEN iTEMS I would like TO OWN
THAT I DON'T...

_____
_____
_____
_____
_____
_____
_____
_____
_____
_____

GO TO A THRIFT SHOP.

DAY 337

TEN ITEMS I WOULD LIKE TO OWN THAT I DON'T ARE...

_____

_____

_____

_____

_____

_____

_____

_____

_____

_____

BUY SLIPPERS.

DAY 338

LIST FIVE THINGS YOU ARE NOT ALLOWED TO DO...

EAT PIE FOR BREAKFAST.

DAY 339

IF I COULD LIGHTEN UP
A LITTLE, I'd LET MYSELF...
("DANCES WITH CATS"?)

_____
_____
_____
_____
_____
_____
_____

MAKE A DOLLHOUSE.

DAY 340

REMEMBER:
YOUR CENSOR'S
NEGATIVE OPINIONS
ARE NOT THE
TRUTH.

YOU CALL THAT DANCE?

LET YOUR ZANY SIDE MAKE DINNER.

DAY 341

PLAY CAN MAKE A WORKAHOLIC
VERY NERVOUS. PLAY IS SCARY.

PLAY JACKS.

DAY 342

MAKE A FANCY "JEWELLED" COLLAR.

DAY 343

MY FAVORITE
WAY TO
DRESS IS...

_____

_____

_____

_____

_____

_____

WEAR PAJAMAS ALL DAY.

DAY 344

LIST
FIVE
IMAGINARY
LIVES.

_____

MAKE SOMETHING OUT OF BEADS.

DAY 345

AS ACTORS WE TEND TO ALLOW
OURSELVES TO BE TYPECAST
RATHER THAN WORKING TO
EXPAND OUR RANGE.

_____

_____

_____

_____

_____

_____

_____

TRY KARAOKE.

DAY 346

SPIRITUAL
BENEFITS
ACCOMPANY
THE PRACTICE
OF A HOBBY.

HOOK A RUG.

DAY 347

Swimming is a wonderful sport for a writer.
The rhythmic, repetitive action transfers the locus of the brain's energies from the logic to the artist hemisphere.

VISIT AN AQUARIUM.

DAY 348

MY FAVORITE
MUSICAL
INSTRUMENT
IS...

GO HEAR INDIAN MUSIC.

DAY 349

SEWING HAS A NICE
WAY OF MENDING UP
PLOTS. AS ARTISTS WE
CAN VERY LITERALLY
REAP WHAT WE SEW.

_____

_____

_____

_____

_____

_____

_____

VISIT A FABRIC SHOP.

DAY 350

TASK: IN A PERFECT WORLD I WOULD SECRETLY LIKE TO...

A TISKET, A TASKET, MY ART FORM IS NOW TYROLEAN BASKETS...

RIDE A CAROUSEL.

DAY 351

AN ARTIST MUST HAVE DOWN TIME. TIME TO DO NOTHING. DEFENDING OUR RIGHT TO SUCH TIME TAKES COURAGE, CONVICTION, RESILIENCY.

READ A CATALOG.

DAY 352

ART NEEDS TIME TO INCUBATE, TO SPRAWL A LITTLE, TO BE UNGAINLY AND MISSHAPEN AND FINALLY EMERGE AS ITSELF.

MAKE PUDDING.

DAY 353

Sunglasses make
THE ARTIST

TAKE YOUR DIVA TO THE MALL.

DAY 354

will MY SCREENPLAY sell...?

RENT CASABLANCA.

DAY 355

HATCHING AN IDEA IS A LOT LIKE BAKING BREAD. AN IDEA NEEDS TIME TO RISE.

_____

_____

_____

_____

_____

MAKE SOMETHING OUT OF STRING.

DAY 356

STAND KNEE-DEEP
IN THE FLOW OF
LIFE AND PLAY
CLOSE ATTENTION.

BUY A HOUSEPLANT.

DAY 357

THE CAPACITY FOR
DELight is THE gift of
PAYING ATTENTION.

GET GREAT SOAP.

DAY 358

WALKING TAKES YOU OUT OF THE PROBLEM & TOWARD THE SOLUTION.

USE YOUR WALKMAN TO WALK.

DAY 359

EXERCISE TEACHES
THE REWARDS OF PROCESS.

MAKE A FRUIT SALAD.

DAY 360

IF MY BODY LOOKED LIKE IT DID TWENTY YEARS AGO, I'D TAKE JAZZERCISE...

OUR USE OF AGE AS A BLOCK TO CREATIVE WORK INTERLOCKS WITH OUR TOXIC FINISHED-PRODUCT THINKING.

FLIMSY EXCUSE!

TAKE AN AFRICAN DANCE CLASS.

DAY 361

what if
Bluebirds
decided
Their songs
weren't good
enough?

MAKE A WREATH.

DAY 362

WRITE AND MAIL AN ENCOURAGING LETTER TO YOUR INNER ARTIST.

WRITE YOURSELF A POEM OF PRAISE.

DAY 363

PUTTING All OUR FEARS
IN A God JAR REAlly
WORKS.

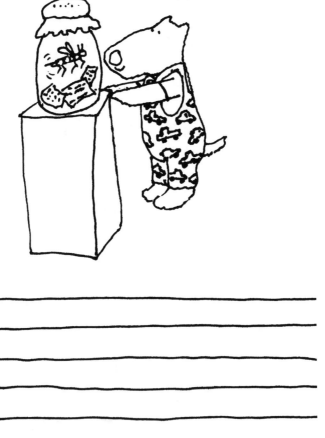

WEAR A SCENTED OiL.

DAY 364

ART MAY NEVER BE FINISHED, BUT AT A CERTAIN POINT YOU LET GO AND CALL IT DONE.

MAKE A PICNIC.

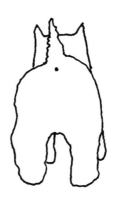

GLOSSARY OF ARTIST'S WAY TERMS AND TOOLS

ARTIST MYTHOLOGY: Artists are an elite tribe of special people (they wear black and live in New York, south of Fourteenth Street) who were born knowing they were real artists, never experience any real self-doubt, are well connected, well recognized, "focused, disciplined, visionary, published, galleried, full time, recognized, famous and rich. . . ." Not like us.

ARTIST DATE: A solitary expedition with your "creative self" into new, interesting, and expansive territory. Expeditions do not need to involve "high art." They might be a trip to an aquarium store, a concert, a used-record store, a drive in the country—anything that "fills the well"—for you. Artist dates are undertaken alone.

ARTIST REALITY: We are all creative, far more creative than we know or acknowledge. It is the process of making art, not the product we produce or its recognition and remuneration, that makes us artists.

ARTIST TRUTH: We are all intended to create. Creativity is our spiritual DNA.

CINEMA SELF: A larger-than-life, movie version of you. This is the silver-screen version where your life has been enlarged, spiffed up, glamorized—in directions you would actually enjoy and approve of ("What kind of car does your Cinema Self drive? What skills does he/she have that you don't yet? What is Cinema Self's signature item of clothing? Who would play Cinema Self in the movie?")

CONSIDER THE ODDS: The phrase most often used by self or others to keep an artist from committing art. (QUESTION: "Yeah, but what are the odds of your selling an original screenplay?" ANSWER: "A lot higher if I do write it!")

CREATIVE CEILING: The often arbitrary and frequently low ceiling that we set for ourselves and our abilities. ("I could never learn to play the piano at my age." "I'm probably not really funny enough to try improv." "I could never learn to sight-read." "I think a novel is just too much for me. . . .")

CREATIVE CHAMPION: Someone who has contributed positive support to you and your creative dreams. ("Of course you can write a novel. You write all the time and I love to read what you write." "Why couldn't you go back to graduate school? Lots of people have." "I don't see why you couldn't go to Italy.")

CREATIVE CLUSTER: A deliberately gathered band of people interested in expanding your and their creativity. Once-weekly meetings, lasting two to three hours, are suggested. (Clusters can also be done by phone or even by letter, but person to person is the most powerful.)

CREATIVE MONSTER: A toxic figure from the past or present who has damaged your self-worth around your creativity. ("This paper is awfully good, John, did someone else write it for you?" "Mary, I don't really know if you have the talent to pursue fine art . . . perhaps a career in teaching?")

EXPANSION MUSIC: The piece of music that most lifts your heart and imagination, allowing you to dream a larger self. This can be anything from Vangelis's "Chariots of Fire," to Mozart, Beethoven, or Rodgers and Hammerstein. Again, this is your piece of "I can do it" music—no one else's.

IMPOSSIBLE DREAM: The act of art we would most like to commit, but tell ourselves we could not possibly accomplish.

MORNING PAGES: Three pages of longhand morning writing. These are strictly steam of consciousness, not "art." They are a Western form of meditation that prioritizes the day, clears and focuses the mind, and offers alternative routing to the solution of many problems.

NARRATIVE TIME LINE: A handwritten stream-of-consciousness autobiography—your life as told to you by you. Fifteen or more pages—often many more. This tool allows you to discover your own version of you, not the official family one we so often—mistakenly—own and parrot. ("Then we moved to that wonderful house in the country. . . ." "Wait a minute! I hated that house. I was lonely. It took me three years to find any friends.")

POISONOUS PLAYMATES: Those people around us, frequently creatively blocked themselves, who undercut our plans for expansion and growth by their own poisonous, well-placed doubts. ("I don't know, hon, you really think you'd be any good at that?")

POSSIBLE DREAM: Same as Impossible Dream. We just need to learn the tools and raise our creative ceiling.

READING DEPRIVATION: A week of media deprivation that allows you to contact—and listen to—your own inner guidance instead of the thoughts, opinions, and guidance of others. Often a threatening concept, reading deprivation is an extremely powerful tool, a kick-start for stalled projects and decisions. For many of us, media is a negative addiction. We glut our own appetite for life with the vicarious experience of others.

SAFETY MUSIC: The piece of music that makes you feel the most safe and protected. This can be anything from Michael Hoppé's "The Yearning" to "Brahms's Lullaby" or "Rock-a-bye Baby" or "Amazing Grace." Do not feel it must be music that anyone else would be impressed by. This is a very idiosyncratic, personal choice.

SECRET SELVES: Inner personas that have a guiding hand in your life decisions, frequently killjoys, but also undervalued positive parts of ourselves. "Do I need to add this cast?" can be in opposition. (Martyred Mary: "I don't think you should let yourself get that coat, it's so expensive." Bon-Bon: "You'll love that coat! Get it and eat tuna fish if you have to!")

SHADOW ARTIST: A person who has used his/her creativity in the service of someone else's art or has chosen a career field parallel to or in service of the real dream. (An artist's manager who really wanted to be an actor, an editor who has always longer to write, etc.).

THE VEIN OF GOLD: That area in which you are most truly yourself and from which your gifts and interests mesh and interact most smoothly and powerfully (e.g., Robert De Niro in movies about male bonding; Kevin Kline in comedies).

WALKING: An invaluable creative tool, used for developing creative ideas, plans, and projects. Next to Morning Pages and Artist Dates, the most potent tool for contracting inner guidance and creativity.

ABOUT THE AUTHOR AND ILLUSTRATOR

JULIA CAMERON has been an active artist for more than thirty years. She is a poet, novelist, playwright, and filmmaker. She has extensive credits in film, television, and theater. Her essays have been anthologized. She has taught and refined for two decades the methods of her bestselling books, The Artist's Way and The Vein of Gold. For the past several years her focus has been on music and sound healing which has informed her award-winning poetry CD, *This Earth*, as well as a metaphysical musical entitled *Avalon.*

A distinguished journalist, she has written for such diverse publications as *The New York Times*, the *Washington Post*, the *Los Angeles Times*, the *Chicago Tribune*, the *Village Voice*, *Rolling Stone*, *American Film*, *Vogue*, and many others. Additionally, she has served on numerous film faculties, including Northwestern University and Columbia College, as well as teaching at such human-potential centers as Esalen, Omega, and the Smithsonian.

ELIZABETH "Libby" CAMERON EVANS works from her studio on her Wisconsin horse farm. She lives with her husband Gary and their horses, cats, and pack of (rescued) dogs.

A graduate of Milwaukee's Layton School of Art and Design, Libby spent nearly nine years at Western Publishing (Golden Books). In 1985, she quit and bought a ticket to Europe. Within three weeks she was discovered by Countess Brenda Cassini on the Spanish Riviera and her portrait painting career was launched.

Her work has appeared in magazines and museums, and she has work in more than five hundred private collections. She is best known for her paintings of horses, dogs, and their owners.

Her "Theo" character was inspired in 1982 by a photo of a West Highland terrier. Libby chose the name "Theo" to honor her sister Julie's support of all artists, as this was the name of Van Gogh's loving brother.

Printed in the United States
by Baker & Taylor Publisher Services